Double Trouble

Activity Book

Name _____

Age _____

Class _____

OXFORD

UNIVERSITY PRESS

Great Clarendon Street, Oxford OX2 6DP

Oxford University Press is a department of the University of Oxford.
It furthers the University's objective of excellence in research, scholarship,
and education by publishing worldwide in

Oxford New York

Auckland Bangkok Buenos Aires Cape Town Chennai
Dar es Salaam Delhi Hong Kong Istanbul Karachi Kolkata
Kuala Lumpur Madrid Melbourne Mexico City Mumbai
Nairobi São Paulo Shanghai Taipei Tokyo Toronto

With offices in

Argentina Austria Brazil Chile Czech Republic France Greece
Guatemala Hungary Italy Japan Poland Portugal Singapore
South Korea Switzerland Thailand Turkey Ukraine Vietnam

OXFORD and OXFORD ENGLISH are registered trade marks of
Oxford University Press in the UK and in certain other countries

ISBN: 978 0 19 440152 4

Printed in China

This book is printed on paper from certified and well-managed sources.

Activities by: Viv Swaine
Illustrations by: Annabel Tempest
Original story by: Craig Wright

Trace and connect.

clock

pencil

angry

happy

park

school

shop

bicycle

1

2

3

4

5

6

7

8

Write.

> tall   policeman   angry
> very   rides   ~~bicycle~~

❶ Sarah has a new ___bicycle___ .

❷ She is _____ happy.

❸ She _____ to the park.

❹ Sarah sees a _____ .

❺ The policeman is _____ .

❻ He is an _____ policeman.

Circle yes **or** no .

❶ Sarah's bicycle is pink.
(yes)
no

❷ Sarah's bicycle is old.
yes
no

❸ She is very angry.
yes
no

❹ She rides to the shops.
yes
no

❺ The policeman is short.
yes
no

❻ The policeman is happy.
yes
no

❼ The policeman says, "Hello!"
yes
no

Connect.

Sarah is going
to the shops. •

Sarah is on
her bicycle. •

Sarah plays
in the park. •

Sarah lives
near the park. •

Sarah's mother
is at home. •

Sarah sits
with her friend
at school. •

Circle the answer.

❶ **What is her name?**

Sarah Simon (Sarah Simms) Sarah Smith

❷ **How old is she?**

six   seven   eight

❸ **Where does she live?**

near the school   near the shops

near the park

❹ **Where is her mother?**

at home   at school   at the shops

❺ **What is her address?**

40 Pine Street   41 Pine Street

14 Pine Street

❻ **What is her telephone number?**

521 8937   521 3789   521 9837

Rearrange the words.

1 address What your is?

<u>What is your address?</u>

2 home at She is.

_____

3 do live you Where?

_____

4 seven am old years I.

_____

5 Simms is My Sarah name.

_____

6 the near live park I.

_____

7 14 address Street is Pine My.

_____

Circle yes or no .

① Sarah is going to school.

yes
no

② It is eight o'clock.

yes
no

③ She has a cat in her bag.

yes
no

④ She has a doll in her bag.

yes
no

⑤ The policeman has
an umbrella.

yes
no

⑥ Sarah has an umbrella.

yes
no

⑦ Bobby and Kevin are
the policeman.

yes
no

⑧ Sarah is angry with
Bobby and Kevin.

yes
no

Write.

❶ _____ hair _____   ❺ _____

❷ _____   ❻ _____

❸ _____   ❼ _____

❹ _____   ❽ _____

Circle each word and write.

❶ (What's)(the)(matter?)

What's the matter?

❷ Whatdoyouhaveinthere?

_____

❸ Ihaveadollandabook.

_____

❹ Iamgoingtomyschool.

_____

❺ CanIgotoschool,now?

_____

❻ AmIintrouble?

_____

❼ Youarenotapoliceman.

_____

Write in alphabetical order.

❶ <u>angry</u>

❷ _____

❸ _____

❹ _____

❺ _____

❻ _____

❼ _____

❽ _____

What page?

1. What is your name? `8`

2. Where is your mother?

3. What time is it?

4. What is your address?

5. Whose bicycle is it?

6. What is this?

7. Where do you live?

8. What's the matter?

Look and write.

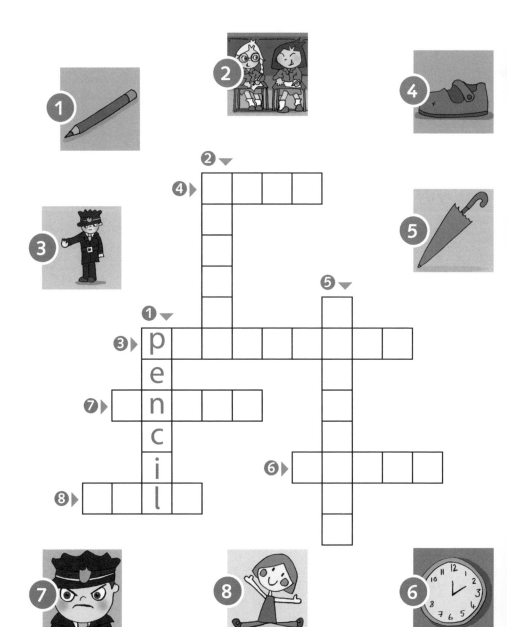

Answer the questions.

❶ What color is Sarah's bicycle?

It is pink.

❷ How old is Sarah?

_____

❸ What is her address?

_____

❹ Where is she going?

_____

❺ Where is her mother?

_____

❻ Where does she live?

_____

❼ What does she have in her bag?

_____

❽ What time is it?

_____

Look and circle.

trouble   telephone   address   mother
surprise   time   number   candy

p	o	i	m	y	t	r	e	w	k	l	k
a	t	r	o	u	b	l	e	o	n	t	v
j	d	e	t	k	w	e	r	p	i	e	y
a	l	l	h	o	m	a	s	d	o	l	f
m	i	e	e	e	i	t	i	o	e	e	n
a	s	u	r	p	r	i	s	e	c	p	u
s	a	h	c	r	k	m	m	l	n	h	m
p	y	a	a	o	i	e	y	e	t	o	b
e	w	n	n	p	a	p	e	r	t	n	e
c	a	d	d	r	e	s	s	f	u	e	r
m	n	b	y	c	x	z	w	u	j	s	n